I0448844

August 2013

VA BENEFITS

Improvements Needed to Ensure Claimants Receive Appropriate Representation

Highlights of GAO-13-643, a report to congressional requesters

VA BENEFITS

Improvements Needed to Ensure Claimants Receive Appropriate Representation

Why GAO Did This Study

Representatives accredited by VA serve a critical role in helping veterans or their family members file claims for VA benefits. By law, accredited individuals must demonstrate good moral character and program knowledge and VA's OGC is tasked to ensure they do so by reviewing initial applications and monitoring ongoing requirements, such as training.

GAO examined (1) the extent to which VA's procedures adequately ensure representatives meet program requirements, and (2) any obstacles that may impede VA's efforts to adequately implement its accreditation process. GAO reviewed relevant federal laws, regulations and procedures, and interviewed VA officials and organizations of accredited representatives. GAO also reviewed a representative sample of accreditation decisions made in 2012 as well as complaints received by VA in 2012. GAO also conducted additional checks on a random but small and non-representative sample of accredited individuals.

What GAO Recommends

To improve the integrity of accreditation, GAO recommends that VA explore options for strengthening knowledge requirements and addressing emerging threats, improve its outreach, and determine the resources needed to adequately carry out accreditation. VA concurred or concurred in principle with GAO's recommendations and cautioned that imposing additional requirements to address concerns with representative knowledge or address emerging threats could have a chilling effect on representation.

View GAO-13-643. For more information, contact Daniel Bertoni at (202) 512-7215 or bertonid@gao.gov.

What GAO Found

The Department of Veterans Affairs' (VA) Office of General Counsel (OGC) procedures do not sufficiently ensure that accredited representatives have good character and knowledge. While GAO's analysis shows that VA follows its procedures for reviewing initial accreditation applications, VA relies on limited self-reported information to determine whether applicants have a criminal history or their character could be called into question, which in turn leaves VA vulnerable to accrediting individuals who may not provide responsible assistance. For example, when GAO conducted additional checks on a non-representative sample of accredited individuals, GAO found that some individuals had histories of bankruptcies or liens, information which could help develop a more complete picture of applicants' character and prompt further inquiry by VA into their background. VA's procedures also do not ensure that representatives have adequate program knowledge. For example, VA's initial training requirements are minimal and VA does not consistently monitor whether representatives meet additional continuing education requirements. As a result, some accredited representatives may not have adequate program knowledge to effectively assist clients with their claims. After being briefed on GAO's findings in May 2013, VA's OGC announced plans to take additional steps toward conducting background checks on applicants and auditing ongoing character and training requirements.

VA efforts to administer accreditation are hindered by an inadequate allocation of resources and unclear communication with claimants. For example, OGC has only four staff dedicated to overseeing thousands of accreditation applications each year, in addition to monitoring approximately 20,000 accredited representatives. As a result, OGC has not kept pace with pending accreditation applications, and has not consistently monitored continuing requirements. OGC's reliance on manual data entry results in resource-intensive program administration. For instance, OGC lacks information technology systems and tools that would help it proactively and efficiently identify representatives who are not meeting ongoing training requirements. Moreover, VA does not clearly solicit feedback from claimants about accredited representatives. For example, neither VA's accreditation web page nor information VA sends to claimants clearly communicates their rights or how to report abuses. Absent such outreach, claimants may not be aware that some representatives may be engaging in prohibited practices. Lastly, VA's current accreditation program does not address some emerging threats to claimants. For instance, VA has received complaints regarding unaccredited individuals inappropriately charging claimants to apply for benefits. By law, only accredited individuals can assist claimants. However, VA is not aware of the extent these unaccredited individuals operate, and is limited in the actions it can take to prevent them from assisting claimants.

Contents

Abbreviations

CLE	Continuing Legal Education
OGC	Office of General Counsel
VA	Department of Veterans Affairs
VBA	Veterans Benefits Administration
VSO	Veteran Service Organization

GAO

U.S. GOVERNMENT ACCOUNTABILITY OFFICE

441 G St. N.W.
Washington, DC 20548

August 1, 2013

Congressional Requesters

In 2012, veterans, their spouses, or survivors filed over a million claims for various benefits with the Department of Veterans Affairs (VA). In order to help these claimants navigate what can be a complex and lengthy process, VA accredits individuals—called representatives—to help ensure responsible and qualified representation is available to prepare, present, and prosecute claims on the behalf of veterans.[1] Representatives who assist veterans and their families in applying for benefits must have good moral character and be capable of providing competent representation, and VA has responsibility for making such determinations through its accreditation process. However, we and others have found instances in which individuals that purport to help veterans may actually be harming them. For example, in prior work we identified instances where representatives charged excessive fees for filing claims or failed to properly file claims, costing veterans thousands of dollars in foregone benefits.[2]

At your request, we reviewed VA's procedures for accrediting and monitoring representatives. Specifically, this report examines (1) the extent to which VA's procedures adequately ensure representatives meet program requirements, and (2) any obstacles that may impede VA's efforts to adequately implement its accreditation process. To identify requirements for the program, we reviewed applicable federal laws, regulations, and program guidance. To determine how VA carries out its responsibilities and the challenges it faces, we interviewed officials in VA's Office of General Counsel—which administers VA's accreditation function—as well as the Veterans Benefits Administration, which reviews disability benefits claims and awards benefits. We also visited a VA regional office to obtain an operational perspective. To gain further understanding of VA's procedures for screening applicants and

---

[1] VA uses the term representative to refer only to individuals affiliated with recognized veteran service organizations, but for the purposes of this report, we use the term more broadly to include all individuals accredited by VA, unless it is specifically stated that we are referring only to representatives of veteran service organizations.

[2] Veterans' Pension Benefits: Improvements Needed to Ensure Only Qualified Veterans and Survivors Receive Benefits, GAO-12-540 (Washington, D.C.: May 15, 2012).

addressing complaints, we reviewed a randomly selected and representative sample of 92 accreditation decisions made in 2012, and a judgmental sample of 24 complaints received by VA. Additionally, we judgmentally selected a sample of 21 individuals—individuals who had either received accreditation in 2012 or individuals for whom VA had received a complaint in 2012—for additional checks into their criminal and financial histories. To provide additional perspectives and further context to our review, we interviewed officials from four national organizations that represent veterans, as well as three organizations that represent accredited attorneys or agents.

We conducted this performance audit from September 2012 to August 2013 in accordance with generally accepted government auditing standards. These standards require that we plan and perform the audit to obtain sufficient, appropriate evidence to provide a reasonable basis for our findings and conclusions based on our audit objectives. We conducted our related investigative work in accordance with investigation standards prescribed by the Council of the Inspectors General on Integrity and Efficiency. Additional information on our scope and methodology is provided in Appendix I.

Background

Although VA is required by law to assist claimants in obtaining the evidence necessary to substantiate a claim for benefits, accreditation helps ensure that claimants have access to qualified representation. By law, only individuals accredited by VA can represent claimants in the VA claims process.[3] Table 1 below describes the three types of individuals that VA recognizes as accredited representatives.

---

[3] VA allows for a one-time exemption so that claimants can designate non-accredited individuals as their representative, without compensation. VA officials told us that this exemption can be used by claimants who wish to designate a family member as their representative.

Table 1: Categories of Individuals Accredited by VA

Category	Who is eligible to apply
Veteran Service Organization (VSO) representatives	Employees or members of recognized veterans service organizations. [a] VSOs are organizations recognized by VA that serve the needs of veterans, such as providing information on benefits and assistance in applying for them. Recognized organizations may be private organizations, as well as state and local government entities.
Attorneys	Attorneys in good standing with a state bar. Any attorney may apply regardless of the area of law in which they specialize.
Claim agents	Any individual who is neither a service organization representative nor an attorney. There is no occupational or educational requirement, but examples include veteran's advocates and financial planners.

Source: GAO analysis of VA regulations and VA.

[a] VA regulations establish a process by which VSOs may be officially recognized by VA. Only recognized VSOs may seek accreditation for their staff or members who wish to provide representation.

To implement accreditation, the law and VA regulations set forth a number of requirements representatives must meet.[4] For example, representatives must:

- *Be of good character:* Although what constitutes good character is not specifically defined, VA regulations provide, with respect to agents and attorneys, that evidence showing a lack of good character and reputation may include such things as: conviction of a felony or other crimes related to fraud, theft, or deceit; or suspension or disbarment from a court, bar, or government agency on ethical grounds. In addition, all representatives are required to be truthful in their dealings with claimants and VA.

- *Provide competent representation:* Representatives must provide competent representation, which includes the knowledge, skills, thoroughness, and preparation necessary for representation, as well as an understanding of the issues of fact and law relevant to the claim.

- *Provide prompt representation:* Representatives must act with reasonable diligence and promptness in representing claimants. This includes responding promptly to VA requests for information or assisting a claimant in responding promptly to VA requests for information.

---

[4] See 38 U.S.C. §§ 5901 - 5905 and 38 C.F.R. §§ 14.626 – 14.637.

GAO-13-643 VA Benefits

As of May 2013, VA had on its rolls approximately 20,000 individuals who are accredited to represent claimants. Specifically, VA had accredited 8,207 VSO representatives, 11,568 attorneys, and 345 claim agents.

Available data demonstrate the growing role and importance of accreditation. Since current program rules were adopted in mid-2008, the number of applications VA received has grown from 2,696 in 2008 to over 5,000 in each year since. Additionally, almost 80 percent of claims that were open as of November 2012 used the services of a representative, with VSOs accounting for the bulk of those claims (see fig. 1).

Figure 1: Number and Percentage of Open Claims by Representation Type

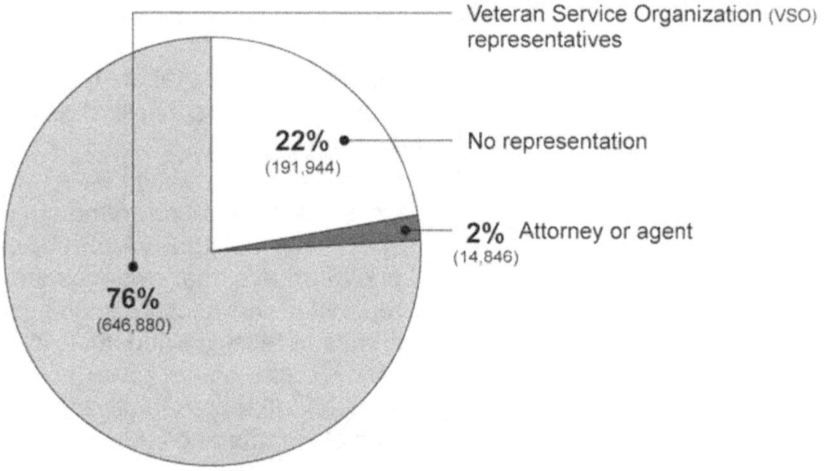

Source: GAO analysis of VA data for claims open on November 30, 2012.

Note: Data provided by VA does not distinguish between attorneys and agents. None reflects claimants who chose to pursue benefits on their own, without the aid of any representative.

VA's Office of General Counsel (OGC) oversees the accreditation program. To this end, OGC staff review accreditation applications and make approval decisions, monitor whether accredited representatives meet ongoing program requirements, and investigate issues and complaints that could lead to a representative having his or her accreditation cancelled or suspended. Table 2 describes the initial and ongoing requirements for these representatives. Additionally, OGC staff receive and review fee agreements—contracts between claimants and representatives outlining how claimants will be charged for services. Within VA, the Veterans Benefits Administration (VBA) also plays a limited role in enforcing accreditation rules—checking that individuals are accredited when claimants designate them as their representative. In cases where an individual is not accredited, VA policy is to inform the would-be representative of accreditation program rules and prohibit the individual from serving as the representative for that claim.

Table 2: Specific Initial and Ongoing Accreditation Requirements by Type of Representative

	Good character requirements		Knowledge requirements	
	Initial	Ongoing	Initial	Ongoing
VSO	VSOs recommending a prospective representative to VA must certify the individual is of good character.	Representatives' good character must be recertified by their VSO every 5 years.	VSOs recommending a prospective representative to VA must certify the individual has demonstrated an ability to represent claimants before VA.	Representatives' ability to represent claimants before VA must be recertified by their VSO every 5 years.
Attorney	Presumed to meet character requirements based on state bar membership in good standing unless OGC receives credible information to the contrary; must also provide character references and background information, including information concerning criminal background, as part of the accreditation application.	Must annually submit to VA information about any court, bar, or federal or state agency to which they are admitted to practice or authorized to appear, along with a certification that they are in good standing.	As a condition of initial accreditation, required to complete 3 hours of qualifying continuing legal education (CLE) within 12 months.	Must complete an additional 3 hours of qualifying CLE within 3 years of initial accreditation and every 2 years thereafter.
Agent	VA must make an affirmative determination of character before a prospective agent can be accredited. Must provide character references and provide background information in application to VA.	Same as ongoing attorney requirements above.	Same as initial attorney requirements above. In addition, must pass a written examination by VA.	Same as ongoing attorney requirements above.

Source: VA regulations and VA.

VA rules also govern the fees that each type of representative can charge claimants. VSO representatives are required to provide their services free of charge. Attorneys and claim agents may not charge claimants for services related to the initial preparation and filing of their claims, but can charge fees for any services rendered after VA makes an initial decision on a claim and the claimant initiates an appeal of VA's decision.[5] For services rendered after an initial decision is made and an appeal is initiated, VA rules generally allow attorneys and agents to charge a

---

[5] For instance, if the claim is denied or claimant believes he or she is entitled to a higher level of disability compensation.

reasonable fee based on retroactive benefits that are awarded. Fees that do not exceed 20 percent of any retroactive benefits are presumed to be reasonable.

VA's OGC may cancel accreditation if the representative fails to meet any of the requirements for accreditation, knowingly presents a fraudulent or frivolous claim, or demands or accepts unlawful compensation. OGC may also suspend and reinstate the individual if he or she meets conditions for reinstatement. Additionally, a VSO can request that VA suspend or cancel accreditation for one of its representatives based on misconduct or lack of competence. OGC is required to inform representatives of the nature of their alleged violation and representatives may request a hearing on the matter. An OGC decision can be appealed to the Board of Veteran's Appeals.

VA's Procedures and Requirements Do Not Sufficiently Ensure That Representatives Are Qualified

VA Does Not Sufficiently Assess Whether Representatives Have Good Character

VA consistently follows its procedures when reviewing applications for accreditation; however, those procedures are not sufficient to ensure representatives have good character.[6] Based on our analysis of a sample of 92 accreditation decisions for attorneys and agents,[7] we estimate that VA correctly followed its procedures in 95 percent of applications

---

[6] VA officials told us they do not have any documented policy or guidance for reviewing applications for accreditation, beyond what is in regulations. In lieu of documented guidance, GAO considered officials' statements made during interviews describing VA's procedures for reviewing applications, and making accreditation decisions as criteria for our review.

[7] Because VA relies on VSOs to certify that their representatives meet requirements for representing veterans, VA's review of accreditation applications and related decisions mostly pertains to attorneys and agents.

approved in 2012.[8] Such procedures include ensuring that applicants have appropriate qualifications (such as bar membership for attorneys), and obtaining additional information when applicants state they had prior criminal activity or other incidents that could call their character into question. That said, we identified several limitations in VA's accreditation procedures and requirements that call into question whether VA can adequately ensure the character of accredited representatives. These include:

Reliance on limited data: VA relies on attorneys and agents to self-report background information on their accreditation applications. For example, these applicants are expected to provide true and correct information about issues such as their criminal history, but VA does not independently verify this information to ensure that applicants were honest about their criminal history. Because they do not verify applicants' information, OGC officials told us they could unknowingly accredit individuals who lack good character. Additionally, VA does not collect additional information, such as Social Security numbers or credit histories, which could be used to conduct a more thorough review of applicants' backgrounds. For instance, when we conducted further inquiries into the backgrounds of accredited attorneys and agents, we found in 9 of 20 instances that individuals had histories of bankruptcies or liens.[9] We also searched to see if these individuals had a criminal history that would warrant further follow-up from VA or had professional licenses suspended, but did not find any such instances. While VA does not currently consider bankruptcies or liens as grounds for barring or cancelling an individual from being accredited, soliciting and confirming such information may provide a more complete picture about an individual's financial situation and management, and could prompt further inquiries that can inform the accreditation decision. The official that oversees accreditation

---

[8] Based on our analysis using a 95 percent confidence interval, VA correctly followed its procedures for 88 to 98 percent of attorney and agent applications approved in 2012. In the remaining cases, there was no evidence in the application file that VA conducted needed follow-up or we were not able to make an assessment because of missing documentation.

[9] For four of these individuals, VA received complaints alleging these same individuals charged non-allowable fees for filing claims. Of the 21 individuals we conducted background checks on, 10 of them had complaints against them on file with VA. The remaining 11 individuals were selected from our sample of 92 attorneys and agents accredited in 2012. We were able to obtain information on 20 of the 21 individuals in our sample.

acknowledged that additional background information, particularly on agents who are also financial planners, would be useful in informing VA's judgment of their character. Subsequent to our May 2013 exit briefing with VA, OGC officials informed us that they recently gained access to VBA's system to conduct background searches and are developing plans to conduct comprehensive background checks on all claim agent applicants and on attorney applicants as necessary. The official that oversees accreditation also stated that VA is considering requiring applicants to supply information on any professional certifications they hold and confirming this information with agencies like the Financial Industry Regulatory Authority, which regulates brokers' activities.

Not consistently following up on references: VA may be missing opportunities to obtain additional information about applicants by not consistently following up on character references. While attorneys and agents are required to provide references in their accreditation applications, the official who oversees accreditation told us that VA contacts references only for agents, which we verified in our review of applications. Further, the value of reference letters VA receives is questionable as VA did not use a standard set of questions or guidance to obtain specific information that should be included in reference letters, such as requesting information on the agents' criminal or employment history. Several reference letters we reviewed did not provide substantial information on applicants' ability to assist veterans. In one instance, VA had to request additional reference letters for an applicant because two of the applicant's reference letters were from members of the same church group and had identical language. Additionally, we found several instances where references listed in applications were family members or lived at the same address as the applicant, calling into question the impartiality of the information received. At our May 2013 exit briefing with VA, officials announced that VA has revised and will begin using a standardized letter to references to specifically request information on agents' criminal and employment histories, as well as their interest in serving veterans.

Reliance on VSOs and state bars: OGC officials told us that they rely heavily on the judgment of VSOs when deciding whether to accredit their prospective representatives. OGC officials told us that they believe VSOs do a good job of screening their applicants and that it is in the best interests of VSOs to maintain a positive reputation regarding the quality of representation they provide as VSOs depend on contributions from veterans to fund their operations. That said, VA does not actively review VSO certification plans and therefore cannot know whether there is variability in procedures and standards among organizations. Regarding attorneys, VA generally presumes good character and fitness to represent claimants if they have a state bar membership in good standing. However, our work shows that an attorney's standing with a state bar may not always be a sufficient proxy for good character. In one example, an attorney was in good standing with his state bar, but he had several previous suspensions from the bar and multiple felonies in his criminal record involving theft or misappropriation of property or funds. In this instance, VA chose not to accredit the individual based on his self-reported criminal record, but it is not clear what the outcome would have been had VA relied on his bar membership status in the absence of such self-reported information.

Limited ongoing monitoring: Once representatives become accredited, VA does little to ensure that they retain good character. VA requires attorneys and agents to annually certify that they are in good standing with any court, bar, or federal or state agency to which they are admitted to practice or authorized to appear. VA also requires VSOs to recertify their representatives every 5 years. However, VA officials told us that they currently face a backlog in processing these annual certifications and therefore have not consistently monitored whether these re-certifications have occurred. For example, the official that oversees accreditation told us that in one instance, an attorney self-reported in a letter to VA that he was disbarred and that his accreditation should be cancelled. Since VA does not consistently monitor whether attorneys annually certify their standing with the bar, the agency would not have known that this individual was disbarred had he not voluntarily communicated this information. After our May 2013 exit briefing with VA, OGC informed us that they are developing plans to annually audit the certifications of good standing that attorneys and agents file.

VA Requirements Do Not Ensure Representatives Are Knowledgeable

VA's initial knowledge requirements for attorneys and agents are limited and do not ensure that they are knowledgeable about VA benefits. To become accredited, agents must pass an exam comprised of 25 multiple-choice and true-false questions. However, organizations that represent or help train agents told us the exam covers a wide array of subjects concerning veterans' benefits law and procedure without deeply broaching any particular topic. Further, they said that the exam alone is not sufficient to determine whether agents have enough knowledge to represent veterans. For attorneys, VA presumes that any attorney in good standing with the bar is qualified and knowledgeable enough to assist veterans. As such, attorneys are not required to take an initial exam to demonstrate their knowledge of veterans' benefits law. However, officials from two organizations that provide training for accreditation told us that membership with the bar does not guarantee that an individual is knowledgeable about VA benefits law. One attorney noted that it can take years to understand VA benefits issues and provide knowledgeable assistance in this area. In fact, representatives from one VSO told us that attorneys and agents often contact VSOs with questions about representing their claimants.

In addition, VA's initial and ongoing training requirements do not ensure accredited attorneys and agents are knowledgeable and VA does not consistently enforce existing requirements. In addition to requiring that attorneys and agents complete 3 hours of qualifying continuing legal education (CLE) within 12 months as an initial condition of accreditation, VA requires that accredited attorneys and agents complete 3 hours of training every 2 years, and that this training cover certain topics such as representation before VA, claims procedures, basic eligibility for benefits, and appeal rights. Officials from two organizations that provide training for accreditation told us that this amount of training is not sufficient to ensure that attorneys and agents are knowledgeable. Additionally, officials from these organizations told us that VA does not review, or provide guidance on course content. OGC officials told us that they rely on each state bar association to approve its own training, which can introduce variability across states. Moreover, VA does not consistently ensure that attorneys and agents complete required training. OGC officials told us that individuals who do not certify their training requirements could have their accreditation suspended. Despite this, OGC has fallen behind on its monitoring of this requirement, and it is likely that individuals who should not be accredited continue to assist claimants. After our May 2013 exit briefing with VA, OGC officials informed us that they are developing plans to annually audit the training certifications which attorneys and agents must file with OGC.

VA relies on VSOs to train their representatives and ensure that VSO representatives can provide knowledgeable assistance to veterans with relatively little oversight from VA. We spoke to three national VSOs who noted that they provide numerous training opportunities for their representatives, which may include on-the-job training, seminars, and regular conferences. Two VSOs we spoke with also said that they monitor whether their representatives are meeting knowledge requirements. However, the official who oversees accreditation said VA relies on VSOs to ensure their staff have appropriate training and that VA does not review VSO training programs. While VA did not express concerns about VSO representatives meeting knowledge requirements, GAO's standards for internal controls state that information about a program's operations should be communicated to management, in order to determine whether the agency is achieving compliance requirements under relevant laws and regulations.[10] Absent better oversight of VSO training, VA cannot ensure the knowledge of representatives who represent a majority of claimants.

Representatives' knowledge is critical to meeting another VA requirement—ensuring that they provide prompt representation. Officials at one regional office noted that some representatives are less knowledgeable than others and that they might forget or overlook certain items in a claim. At the same time, they stated that it is VA's responsibility to review claims to make sure they are complete and to notify claimants when information is missing. However, officials from an organization representing attorneys and agents told us that VA does not consistently follow up with veterans to make sure that their paperwork is complete and there have been instances where mistakes on initial claims resulted in veterans losing the ability to claim benefits that they were entitled to receive. Similarly, the officials told us that a representative who is not knowledgeable enough to use the appropriate language for appealing a decision may result in VA not recognizing the communication as a formal disagreement with VA's decision, in turn causing the veteran to miss the deadline for appealing their claims case.

---

[10] The standards for internal control emphasize the need for agencies to have relevant and reliable information relating to external as well as internal events, in order to run and control operations. To support agencies' efforts to obtain information, the internal controls specifically state that operational information should be provided to managers so that they may determine whether their programs comply with applicable laws and regulations. See GAO, *Internal Control Management and Evaluation Tool,* GAO-01-1008G (Washington, D.C.: August 2001) and GAO, *Standards for Internal Control in the Federal Government,* GAO/AIMD-00-21.3.1 (Washington, D.C.: November 1999).

Inadequate Resource Allocation and Unclear Communication with Claimants Hinder Efforts to Administer Accreditation

Inadequate Staffing and Information Technology Leads to Backlogs and Limited Program Monitoring

VA has dedicated only a few staff to administer its accreditation program, which has resulted in limited monitoring efforts and workload backlogs. VA officials told us that approximately four staff positions in OGC are dedicated to accreditation. These staff are responsible for reviewing thousands of applications each year, and ensuring that the approximately 20,000 individuals already accredited meet continuing requirements. Officials told us this level of staffing is insufficient to carry out all these responsibilities and that VA has chosen to prioritize screening initial accreditation applications over monitoring ongoing requirements. Even so, VA has a significant backlog of accreditation applications to review. VA estimates that it may take 60 to 120 days to review an application after it is received. Because by law only accredited individuals may represent claimants, this backlog may cause delays for claimants who need assistance with their claims.

VA currently has no plans to permanently increase the number of staff dedicated to accreditation. OGC officials told us that they have been seeking to increase the number of staff working on accreditation, but have been unsuccessful in obtaining additional permanent staff. An official noted that in the fall of 2012, several staff were assigned to accreditation on a temporary basis and, with their help, OGC was able to eliminate its backlog of attorney and VSO representative applications. However, OGC stated that a considerable backlog of agent applications remains and it is likely the backlog of attorney and VSO representative applications will return since this temporary initiative has ended. Moreover, as of May 2013, one of the four positions was not filled because of a resignation. OGC is in the process of replacing staff lost to attrition as well as obtaining an additional temporary staff person. Still, OGC officials stated that they would need several additional staff beyond the four dedicated positions to function more effectively. It is questionable if this will happen in the near future as VA's proposed fiscal year 2014 budget calls for fewer staff in VA's OGC. This may also affect OGC's plans to increase its oversight of accredited representatives because those plans are contingent upon eliminating the backlog of initial applications.

VA's implementation of its accreditation process is also hampered by limited information technology (IT) support. Officials told us that the database system used by OGC cannot automatically inform individuals that they are meeting program requirements and OGC staff must do this manually. Further, an official noted that a significant amount of data entry is required when applicants submit information for accreditation. Officials noted that other IT improvements, such as the ability for applicants to electronically submit applications, or for accredited representatives to submit certifications of good standing and training certifications would help OGC manage its responsibilities more efficiently. However, no steps have been taken to date toward developing these capabilities.

VA's Oversight Is Limited by a Lack of Outreach to Claimants and an Unclear Complaint Process

VA's ability to identify and address abuses by representatives is limited because VA has missed opportunities to educate claimants about their rights and protections against potential abuses. In prior work, we reported that targeted communication with a specific message is a best practice for outreach to veterans.[11] Individuals who do not yet have representation receive a letter from VA after submitting a claim containing some information on representation—such as explaining what VSOs are and that they provide assistance at no charge. However, the letter does not discuss attorneys and agents, nor does it note that a claimant should not have to pay for services associated with filing an initial claim. Similarly, the form that claimants use to designate an attorney or agent[12] refers individuals to the section of the law governing fees, but does not explain that claimants should not pay for filing an initial claim. Beyond these forms, VBA officials told us that VA does not actively conduct outreach to claimants regarding representation, what to expect from their representative, or their right to not pay filing fees for initial claims. As a

---

[11] GAO, *Social Security Disability: Additional Outreach and Collaboration on Sharing Medical Records Would Improve Wounded Warriors' Access to Benefits*, GAO-09-762 (Washington, D.C.: Sept. 16, 2009).

[12] VA requires a signed declaration of representation designating the representative on VA Form 21-22 or 21-22a before an individual can represent a claimant.

result, several VSOs we interviewed stated that veterans are often unaware of their rights or what to expect during the claims process. One VSO service officer told us that nearly all veterans he encounters are unaware that they should not pay to file initial claims. He added that if a veteran is told that he or she must pay a fee, the veteran will usually just assume this is how business is done. Further, many of the complaints to VA we reviewed regarded improper fees.

VA's ability to learn about and address potential abuses also may be hampered by a complaint process that is not well-communicated to claimants. GAO standards for internal controls state that effective communications—such as with external stakeholders—is critical for agencies to ensure they receive information that may significantly affect whether they achieve their objectives. While VA regulations establish a complaint process, VA may be missing opportunities to serve and protect claimants as it has not clearly communicated to claimants or others how to report concerns about representatives.[13] For example, VA's accreditation website does not explicitly state how to report concerns about representatives. While the website provides a link to an e-mail address used for general inquiries, an official noted that OGC receives a large volume of emails at this address—including complaints—and is behind in responding to inquiries. Additionally, the materials provided to individuals when filing a claim also do not clearly state how to report complaints. When we interviewed veterans at two VSOs in the D.C. area, we generally found that they were unfamiliar with program requirements and did not know where or how to file a complaint.

Further, the process of responding to and addressing complaints—which can be difficult and lengthy—is understaffed, thereby limiting its effectiveness. VA officials told us they require clear and convincing evidence in order to cancel a representative's accreditation. One official noted the process of monitoring representatives who received complaints is difficult given competing demands for resources. Additionally, collecting evidence can be difficult because claimants may be reluctant to reveal their identities when making complaints. They added that some cancellation actions may take years to resolve when representatives exercise their right to appeal decisions. An OGC official told us that

---

[13] VA's regulations clearly indicate that OGC will accept credible written information from any source indicating improper conduct or incompetence on the part of representatives of any kind.

allocated resources were currently inadequate to effectively monitor representatives about whom complaints had been submitted and that information about complaints is not shared with other parts of VA. For instance, OGC does not share information with VBA that could help identify or monitor the activities of representatives with complaints. OGC estimated that only two attorneys or agents had their accreditation cancelled over the last 5 years for violating the rules of the program and none were suspended.[14]

Accreditation Does Not Address Some Emerging Threats

VA faces challenges with unaccredited individuals helping veterans file claims and charging claimants for assistance. While federal regulations require representatives to be accredited, we found a number of complaints about individuals who are not accredited filing claims for veterans. Of the 24 complaints filed against attorneys and agents in 2012, 7 were regarding unaccredited individuals. Because VA is not aware of the extent to which these individuals interact with claimants, VA cannot take action or ensure they provide quality services. An OGC official told us that when it learns of these individuals, it is limited in the actions it can take beyond instructing the individual to stop. Additionally, he said he has written to state attorneys general offices regarding potential wrongful actions a few times in the last year, but does not know if the states took action. In our review, we found a few instances in which OGC sent letters concerning unaccredited individuals to state attorneys general only to continue to receive complaints about these individuals. An OGC official added that, beyond cancelling or suspending accreditation, there are no penalties for individuals who violate the requirements of accreditation and that cases generally are not referred to VA's Inspector General.

Accreditation also does not address whether individuals should sell financial products to veterans. Our prior work has shown that some accredited individuals were selling financial products to veterans in order

---

[14] In this same time period, VA estimates that 17 VSO representatives lost their accreditation for breaking program rules and 3 were suspended. Officials told us that VSOs may request that VA cancel accreditation for their representatives based on their own information regarding the individual's behavior. Many more individuals have their accreditation cancelled for reasons not related to conduct. VA estimates that 1,387 VSO representatives, 15 attorneys, and 1 agent had their accreditation cancelled for reasons not related to conduct in fiscal year 2012.

to shelter assets and allow them to qualify for VA pension benefits.[15] Some of these cases involved vulnerable populations, such as veterans in assisted living facilities, or involved individuals selling products that resulted in veterans losing control of their assets without qualifying for VA benefits. VA and some VSO officials told us that financial planners continue to be an area of concern. VA officials told us that an increasing number of financial planners are applying for accreditation as agents. In fact, all six of the agents in our file review appeared to have a financial planning background. VA also told us that when an individual with a financial planning background applies for accreditation, it asks for additional information about their business plans, reviews any business websites, and reminds applicants that the purpose of accreditation is to provide assistance to veterans and that they should not use accreditation to promote financial products. That said, the official who oversees accreditation told us that they often lack a sufficient basis to deny accreditation to these individuals because being a financial planner in and of itself does not violate VA's accreditation rules. He added that it might be helpful to collect additional information on these individuals, such as from financial regulators, when deciding whether to accredit them.

It is also difficult for VA to ensure that claimants are being charged appropriate fees. Attorneys and agents are not allowed to charge or receive a fee for the preparation or initial filing of a claim, but are allowed to charge a fee for services provided after VA has decided the claim and a notice of disagreement has been filed initiating an appeal of that decision. The allowable fee is often 20 percent of retroactive benefits awarded if the claim is granted. However, there is no restriction on fees charged for services before an individual files a claim. VA's OGC issued a letter in 2004 noting that attorneys may charge claimants for services that are rendered before the individual begins the process of filing a claim, such as consulting with the individual about the range of VA and other federal benefits he or she may qualify for. Some VSOs and other experts expressed some concern regarding pre-filing consultation fees. The head of one VSO noted that these fees may serve as a mechanism to hide the fact that attorneys and agents are charging claimants for preparing

---

[15] VA pension benefits are intended to provide economic benefits to low-income veterans who served during a time of war, and to qualify, veterans must have income and assets below a certain threshold. Our prior work found instances of companies advertising financial planning services to veterans that circumvented eligibility requirements such as by placing assets in trusts or transferring them to family members. See GAO-12-540.

claims. Ambiguity regarding these fees makes it difficult for claimants and VA to know whether they are being charged allowable fees, and may result in attorneys inappropriately billing for work related to the claim as if it was for a general consultation. Because fees for pre-filing activities are outside the claims process, VA also has no way of knowing the extent to which they occur or are properly charged. More than half of the complaints against attorneys and agents (15 of 24) that we reviewed were related to fees.

Conclusions

Hundreds of thousands of veterans and their families rely on accredited representatives to guide them through the process of applying for VA benefits. However, current program implementation and requirements do not sufficiently ensure that veterans and their families are protected against potential abuses or that VA has the ability to identify and address situations where representatives are not acting in the best interests of clients. While recent plans to collect more information on applicants and increase oversight of existing representatives are promising, it is unclear how OGC will implement and sustain these improvements given the current level of resources VA has allocated to this program. Additionally, without providing better information to claimants about how to report issues or concerns about their representation, claimants may not know where to turn to report an abuse or not even recognize that their representative is engaged in prohibited practices. Lastly, claimants may be vulnerable to emerging threats—such as unaccredited representatives—in the absence of VA tools to provide protection. We recognize that in considering program enhancements, VA will need to balance the effort of instituting changes and the additional burdens they may place on program staff and representatives with ensuring that claimants continue to have ready access to representation. However, representatives with ill-intent or poor knowledge can cause real harm to claimants and a weak accreditation process will negatively affect VA's ability to provide veterans the benefits to which they are entitled.

Recommendations for Executive Action

To improve VA's ability to ensure that claimants are represented by qualified and responsible individuals, the Secretary of Veterans Affairs should explore options and take steps to:

1. Ensure an appropriate level of staff and IT resources are in place to implement the requirements of the accreditation program. This should include exploring options for utilizing other VA components and resources outside of OGC.

2. Strengthen initial and continuing knowledge requirements for accreditation for all types of representatives.

3. Enhance communications with claimants, including how they can report complaints related to their representation. This could include exploring options for incorporating information about representation and veterans' rights into existing communications and outreach efforts.

4. Address potentially abusive practices by representatives who lack accreditation, charge inappropriate fees, or sell financial products to claimants that are not in their best interest. If necessary, VA should consider seeking additional legislative authority to address such practices and enforce program rules.

Agency Comments and Our Evaluation

We provided a draft of this report to the Secretary of Veterans Affairs for review and comment. In its comments (see app. II), VA generally agreed with our conclusions, and either concurred or concurred in principle or in part with our recommendations, as discussed more fully below.

VA concurred in principle with our first recommendation to ensure accreditation has appropriate staffing and IT resources, noting that efforts to increase staff and obtain IT resources must be considered within the existing OGC budget. We agree and fully support VA's plans to identify available resources within and outside of OGC.

VA concurred in principle with our second recommendation that it explore strengthening initial and continuing knowledge requirements. VA stated that it believes that existing initial knowledge requirements for attorneys and agents adequately ensure that VA claimants have qualified representation. Additionally, VA expressed concerns that additional knowledge or testing requirements could have a chilling effect on attorney representation for claimants. Nevertheless, VA stated that it will consider ways in which it can equip newly accredited attorneys and agents with information regarding veterans benefits law and procedures. Additionally, VA stated it plans to revise and update examinations for prospective agents to ensure they have adequate knowledge of veterans law and procedures. Regarding VSO representatives, VA reiterated that it believes it is in each organization's best interest to ensure their representatives are competent and qualified. Nevertheless, VA plans to request and review training curricula for up to about 10 percent of recognized organizations each year—an effort which we commend. We support these efforts, but continue to believe VA should consider ways to better equip all accredited attorneys and agents with relevant information and not limit efforts to just newly accredited attorneys and agents, for example, by improving the quality of required continuing legal education.

Regarding our recommendation to enhance communications with claimants, VA concurred and plans to include information on how to report complaints on OGC's accreditation Web site, and will work with VBA to identify potential outreach activities. We agree with VA's stated efforts to improve communication with claimants.

VA also concurred in principle with our recommendation to explore options for addressing potentially abusive practices by representatives and stated it would consider seeking additional legislative authority to address these practices and enforce program rules. VA noted that imposing penalties on unaccredited individuals, individuals who inappropriately charge claimants, or sell financial products to claimants could help curb inappropriate practices, but in some cases may have a chilling effect on the legitimate activities of others. We acknowledge that penalties may be an appropriate deterrent in some but not all circumstances and agree with VA's desire to balance any changes with maintaining access for claimants to valuable assistance. We also urge VA to further explore other remedies that would not require legislative action, such as closer cooperation with state and local law enforcement regarding individuals who may commit unlawful acts.

As agreed with your offices, unless you publicly announce the contents of this report earlier, we plan no further distribution until 30 days from the report date. At that time, we will send copies of this report to the appropriate congressional committees, the Secretary of Veterans Affairs, and other interested parties. In addition, this document will be available at no charge on GAO's Web site at http://www.gao.gov.

If you or your staff have any questions about this report, please contact me at (202) 512-7215 or at bertonid@gao.gov. Contact points for our Offices of Congressional Relations and Public Affairs may be found on the last page of this report. Staff members who made key contributions to this report are listed in Appendix III.

Daniel Bertoni
Director, Education, Workforce,
   and Income Security

List of Requesters

The Honorable Patty Murray
Chairman
Committee on the Budget
United States Senate

The Honorable Bernie Sanders
Chairman
The Honorable Richard Burr
Ranking Member
Committee on Veterans' Affairs
United States Senate

The Honorable Bill Nelson
Chairman
Special Committee on Aging
United States Senate

Appendix I: Objectives, Scope, and Methodology

In conducting our review of how the Department of Veterans Affairs (VA) accredits and oversees veterans' representatives, our objectives were to examine (1) the extent to which VA's procedures adequately ensure representatives meet program requirements, and (2) any obstacles that may impede VA's effort to adequately implement its accreditation process. We conducted this performance audit from September 2012 to August 2013, in accordance with generally accepted government auditing standards. These standards require that we plan and perform the audit to obtain sufficient, appropriate evidence to provide a reasonable basis for our findings and conclusions based on our audit objectives. We believe the evidence obtained provides a reasonable basis for our findings and conclusions based on our audit objectives. We conducted our related investigative work in accordance with investigation standards prescribed by the Council of the Inspectors General on Integrity and Efficiency.

To determine the extent to which VA's procedures are adequate, we reviewed pertinent federal laws and regulations and interviewed officials in VA's Office of General Counsel (OGC) and Veterans Benefits Administration. To assess the extent to which VA carries out its procedures, we reviewed a random, representative sample of 92 case files for attorneys and agents who were granted accreditation in 2012.[1] We examined these files to determine whether individuals provided complete information on their personal histories, whether individuals had the appropriate qualifications, and to determine whether VA took steps to collect additional information when necessary. We determined whether the evidence in each file indicated that VA carried out the procedures that VA officials stated they follow when reviewing files.[2] Additionally, we reviewed all 24 complaints that OGC received in 2012 regarding attorneys and claim agents in order to understand the actions that VA takes in response to concerns. Additionally, we selected a random, judgmental sample of 21 attorneys and agents to determine whether an independent background check would uncover issues that could call their character into question. These 21 individuals consisted of 5 attorneys and 6 agents selected in our random sample of 2012 accreditation decisions,

---

[1] We decided to not review accreditation decisions for Veterans' Service Organization representatives since VA officials told us that they generally rely on the recommendation of the organizations when approving these applications.

[2] We found incomplete documentation or missing documents in 3 of the 92 files selected. In these cases, we were not able to determine whether VA carried out its procedures.

and 5 attorneys and 5 agents whose complaint files we reviewed.[3] We
used Accurint—a commercial database of public records—to determine
whether these individuals had (1) a criminal history, (2) bankruptcies, (3)
liens, or (4) professional licenses revoked. In the instances in which
Accurint delivered a positive result, we confirmed the result by obtaining
court records.

To provide further context on VA's procedures and to determine obstacles
that impede VA's efforts to adequately implement accreditation, we
interviewed a number of veterans service organizations (VSO)—which
both assist veterans in filing claims and advocate for their interests—and
organizations that represent attorneys and claim agents (see table 3).

Table 3: Organizations Interviewed by GAO

Veterans service organizations	Groups representing attorneys or agents
• American Legion	• Academy of VA Pension Planners
• Disabled American Veterans	• National Care Planning Council
• National Veterans Legal Services Program	• National Organization of Veterans' Advocates
• Veterans of Foreign Wars	

Source: GAO.

Additionally, we conducted a site visit to the Philadelphia VA Regional
Office where we interviewed regional managers, veterans service
representatives, and staff who review fee agreements, as well as local
VSO representatives. Finally, we informally met with groups of veterans
who were present at two VSOs in the Washington, D.C. area on the days
of our visits, to obtain views on their experiences with representation.

---

[3] Our search did not find results for 1 individual, so we reported on findings for the
remaining 20 in our report.

DEPARTMENT OF VETERANS AFFAIRS
Washington, DC 20420

July 10, 2013

Mr. Daniel Bertoni
Director, Education, Workforce, and
 Income Security Issues
U.S. Government Accountability Office
441 G Street, NW
Washington, DC 20548

Dear Mr. Bertoni:

The Department of Veterans Affairs (VA) has reviewed the Government Accountability Office's (GAO) draft report, *"VA BENEFITS: Improvements Needed to Ensure Claimants Receive Appropriate Representation"* (GAO-13-643). VA generally agrees with GAO's conclusions and concurs in principle with recommendation 1, concurs in part with recommendation 2, and concurs with GAO's recommendations 3 and 4, to the Department.

The enclosure specifically addresses GAO's recommendations and provides technical comments to the draft report. VA appreciates the opportunity to comment on your draft report.

Sincerely,

Jose D. Riojas
Interim Chief of Staff

Enclosure

Department of Veterans Affairs (VA) Comments to
Government Accountability Office (GAO) Draft Report
*"VA BENEFITS: Improvements Needed to Ensure Claimants Receive
Appropriate Representation"*
(GAO-13-643)

GAO Recommendation: To improve VA's ability to ensure that claimants are
represented by qualified and responsible individuals, the Secretary of Veterans
Affairs should explore options and take steps to:

Recommendation 1: Ensure an appropriate level of staff and IT resources are in
place to implement the requirements of the accreditation program. This should
include exploring options for utilizing other VA components and resources
outside of OGC.

VA Comment: Concur in principle. Although the Department of Veterans Affairs (VA)
agrees that it would be beneficial for the Office of General Counsel (OGC) to increase
its staff and obtain additional Information Technology (IT) support to implement the
requirements of the accreditation program, this recommendation must be considered
within the existing OGC budget. VA will continue to explore staffing and IT options
within and outside of OGC.

Recommendation 2: Strengthen initial and continuing knowledge requirements
for accreditation for all types of representatives.

VA Comment: Concur in principle. Section 5904(a)(2) of title 38, United States Code
(U.S.C.), requires VA to prescribe in regulations a requirement that, as a condition of
accreditation as an agent or attorney, an individual must have either a specific level of
experience or specialized training. An applicant for accreditation as either an attorney
or agent "must establish that he or she is of good character and reputation, is qualified
to render valuable assistance to claimants, and is otherwise competent to advise and
assist claimants in the preparation, presentation, and prosecution of their claim(s)
before VA." 38 Code of Federal Regulations (CFR) § 14.629(b)(2).

With regard to strengthening initial knowledge requirements for accreditation for
attorneys, VA believes that the current requirements adequately ensure qualified
representation of VA claimants. As part of their initial accreditation requirements,
attorneys must have a law degree, be a member in good standing of a state bar, and,
during the first 12-month period following initial accreditation, complete 3 hours of
state-bar approved Continuing Legal Education (CLE) training covering Veterans
benefits law and procedure. To impose additional testing or knowledge requirements
on attorneys may have a chilling effect on attorney representation for VA claimants, in
particular pro bono representation of indigent Veterans. We believe that, generally, the
formal education and testing already required of licensed attorneys, attorneys' ethical
responsibilities concerning representation, along with VA's CLE requirements,
adequately balance the competing interests of ensuring qualified representation with
facilitating choice of representation for VA claimants. However, VA will consider ways in

1

Enclosure

Department of Veterans Affairs (VA) Comments to
Government Accountability Office (GAO) Draft Report
*"VA BENEFITS: Improvements Needed to Ensure Claimants Receive Appropriate
Representation"*
(GAO-13-643)

which we may be able to equip newly accredited attorneys with information regarding
Veterans benefits law and procedures.

With regard to strengthening initial knowledge requirements for accreditation for agents,
VA believes that the current requirements adequately ensure qualified representation of
VA claimants. As part of their initial accreditation requirements, agents must pass a
written examination administered by VA, which covers a wide range of topics covering
the applicant's knowledge of VA benefits and the VA claims adjudication process, and
complete the same CLE training as attorneys. 38 CFR § 14.629(b). The sole purpose
of VA's accreditation examination is to objectively determine whether an agent has the
qualifications necessary to provide competent representation before VA. VA continues
to believe that examinations are necessary for agent applicants because they have not
completed similar legal training as attorneys or passed a state-bar administered
examination. However, VA plans to revise and update our examinations to further
ensure that they are adequately testing an agent applicant's knowledge of current
Veterans' benefits law and procedure. As with attorneys, VA will also consider ways in
which VA may be able to equip newly accredited agents with information regarding
Veterans benefits law and procedures.

As GAO notes in its report, in order to strengthen continuing knowledge requirements
for accreditation for attorneys and agents, OGC plans to annually audit the training
certifications which attorneys and agents must file with OGC to ensure timely and
adequate submissions. In light of OGC's limited resources, VA believes this new audit
plan will sufficiently hold accredited attorneys and agents accountable in completing
necessary CLE training on Veterans benefits law and procedures to maintain VA's
accreditation.

With regard to Veterans Service Organization (VSO) representatives, VA relies heavily
on the organizations to provide adequate training for their representatives. We believe
it is within each organization's interest to ensure that its accredited representatives are
competent and qualified to represent claimants before VA. For each individual a VSO
desires accredited as a representative of that organization, the VSO must certify that
the individual "has demonstrated an ability to represent claimants before VA."
38 CFR § 14.629(a). VA currently does not have the resources to review screening
procedures and training curricula for 92 VA-recognized organizations. However, VA
plans to request and review training curricula for up to nine organizations every year to
ensure that they provide adequate training for their representatives.

To the extent VA receives complaints regarding the qualifications or competence of
specific accredited attorneys, agents, or VSO representatives, we have procedures in

2

Enclosure

Department of Veterans Affairs (VA) Comments to
Government Accountability Office (GAO) Draft Report
*"VA BENEFITS: Improvements Needed to Ensure Claimants Receive Appropriate
Representation"*
(GAO-13-643)

place to initiate inquiries and proceedings to suspend or cancel their accreditation.
38 CFR § 14.633.

Recommendation 3: Enhance communications with claimants, including how
they can report complaints related to their representation. This could include
exploring options for incorporating information about representation and
veterans' rights into existing communications and outreach efforts.

VA Comment: Concur. VA plans to add information on OGC's public accreditation
Web site about how to report complaints to OGC regarding unlawful or unethical
practices or incompetent representation by accredited individuals. Complaints could
also include information regarding an accredited individual's suspension or disbarment
by any court, bar, or Federal or state agency to which such individual was previously
admitted to practice. OGC will work with the Veterans Benefits Administration on
identifying potential outreach opportunities.

Recommendation 4: Address potentially abusive practices by representatives
who lack accreditation, charge inappropriate fees, or sell financial products to
claimants that are not in their best interest. If necessary, VA should consider
seeking additional legislative authority to address such practices and enforce
program rules.

VA Comment: Concur in principle. VA will consider seeking additional legislative
authority to address abusive practices and enforce program rules. (Any such legislative
proposals would require Executive Branch clearance.)

Currently, if VA determines that an unaccredited individual is assisting claimants with
their claims for VA benefits, VA may notify such individual to cease the unlawful
practice. VA will not recognize an unaccredited individual as a claimant's
representative. There are, however, no penalties under Federal law for assisting a
claimant in the preparation, presentation, or prosecution of a claim without accreditation.
Legislation that would impose penalties on unaccredited individuals who assist
claimants with their claims for VA benefits could potentially help reduce this unlawful
practice. However, such legislation might also penalize the acts of well-intentioned
unaccredited individuals who assist claimants without knowledge of the laws against
such practice. It may also have an unintended chilling effect on individuals who want to
assist Veterans in other capacities, such as by merely educating claimants about the
benefits that might be available to them, which does not require VA accreditation.

3

Enclosure

Department of Veterans Affairs (VA) Comments to
Government Accountability Office (GAO) Draft Report
"VA BENEFITS: Improvements Needed to Ensure Claimants Receive Appropriate
Representation"
(GAO-13-643)

Currently, if VA determines that an accredited or unaccredited individual is charging a
fee for assisting claimants with applications for VA benefits, VA may notify such
individual to cease the unlawful practice. If VA determines that an accredited individual
is improperly charging a fee for preparing, presenting, or prosecuting a claim prior to the
filing of a notice of disagreement with a VA regional office decision, VA may suspend or
cancel the individual's accreditation. If an unaccredited individual fails to cease the
unlawful practice, VA will report the individual to state or local agencies or offices that
enforce unauthorized practice, unfair business practice, or consumer or senior fraud
laws. There are, however, no criminal penalties under Federal law for unlawfully
charging a fee for assisting a claimant with an application for VA benefits. Legislation
that would impose penalties on accredited and unaccredited individuals who charge a
fee for assisting claimants with their applications for VA benefits could potentially help
curb this unlawful practice. Under former 38 U.S.C. § 5905(1) (2002), it was a
misdemeanor to solicit or charge fees for assisting a claimant with a claim for VA
benefits before an initial decision by the Board of Veterans' Appeals. However,
Congress repealed this provision in December 2006 with the enactment of Public Law
109-461, most likely to encourage representation of claimants in their claims for VA
benefits.

Currently, as noted in the GAO report, when an individual with a financial planning
background applies for accreditation, VA asks for additional information about their
business plans, review any business Web sites, and make it clear that VA does not
accredit individuals for the purpose of promoting their other business interests involving
insurance, annuities, or other financial products. VA informs them that if we learn that
an accredited individual is using VA accreditation for a purpose other than assisting in
the preparation, presentation, and prosecution of a claim, VA will consider suspending
or cancelling his or her accreditation. As further noted in the GAO report, VA often
lacks a sufficient basis to deny accreditation to these individuals because being a
financial planner in and of itself does not violate VA's accreditation rules. VA does not
have authority to preclude VA-accredited representatives, agents, or attorneys from
selling financial products to claimants—they simply cannot use their accreditation for
that purpose. However, VA is considering requiring applicants to submit information on
any professional certifications they hold and confirming this information with agencies
like the Financial Industry Regulatory Authority. Although VA informs applicants for
accreditation that it is unlawful to use VA accreditation for the purpose of promoting or
selling financial products, in practice, it is difficult to assess when that is actually
occurring. Legislation that would impose penalties on accredited individuals who sell
financial products to claimants may help deter such individuals from using their
accreditation to sell financial products to claimants. However, such legislation may
deter well-intentioned individuals from pursuing accreditation to assist Veterans and

4

Enclosure

Department of Veterans Affairs (VA) Comments to
Government Accountability Office (GAO) Draft Report
*"VA BENEFITS: Improvements Needed to Ensure Claimants Receive Appropriate
Representation"*
(GAO-13-643)

may also deprive claimants of opportunities to learn of financial products that would be beneficial to them.

5

Appendix III: GAO Contact and Staff Acknowledgments

GAO Contact	Daniel Bertoni, (202) 512-7215 or bertonid@gao.gov.
Staff Acknowledgments	In addition to the contact named above, Michele Grgich and Lori Rectanus (Assistant Directors), Daniel Concepcion and Aimee Elivert made key contributions to this report. David Chrisinger, Paul Desaulniers, Sheila McCoy, Wayne McElrath, Dae Park, Almeta Spencer, Roger Thomas, and Walter Vance provided support.

GAO's Mission	The Government Accountability Office, the audit, evaluation, and investigative arm of Congress, exists to support Congress in meeting its constitutional responsibilities and to help improve the performance and accountability of the federal government for the American people. GAO examines the use of public funds; evaluates federal programs and policies; and provides analyses, recommendations, and other assistance to help Congress make informed oversight, policy, and funding decisions. GAO's commitment to good government is reflected in its core values of accountability, integrity, and reliability.
Obtaining Copies of GAO Reports and Testimony	The fastest and easiest way to obtain copies of GAO documents at no cost is through GAO's website (http://www.gao.gov). Each weekday afternoon, GAO posts on its website newly released reports, testimony, and correspondence. To have GAO e-mail you a list of newly posted products, go to http://www.gao.gov and select "E-mail Updates."
Order by Phone	The price of each GAO publication reflects GAO's actual cost of production and distribution and depends on the number of pages in the publication and whether the publication is printed in color or black and white. Pricing and ordering information is posted on GAO's website, http://www.gao.gov/ordering.htm.
	Place orders by calling (202) 512-6000, toll free (866) 801-7077, or TDD (202) 512-2537.
	Orders may be paid for using American Express, Discover Card, MasterCard, Visa, check, or money order. Call for additional information.
Connect with GAO	Connect with GAO on Facebook, Flickr, Twitter, and YouTube. Subscribe to our RSS Feeds or E-mail Updates. Listen to our Podcasts. Visit GAO on the web at www.gao.gov.
To Report Fraud, Waste, and Abuse in Federal Programs	Contact: Website: http://www.gao.gov/fraudnet/fraudnet.htm E-mail: fraudnet@gao.gov Automated answering system: (800) 424-5454 or (202) 512-7470
Congressional Relations	Katherine Siggerud, Managing Director, siggerudk@gao.gov, (202) 512-4400, U.S. Government Accountability Office, 441 G Street NW, Room 7125, Washington, DC 20548
Public Affairs	Chuck Young, Managing Director, youngc1@gao.gov, (202) 512-4800 U.S. Government Accountability Office, 441 G Street NW, Room 7149 Washington, DC 20548

Please Print on Recycled Paper.